From Hurt to Healed:
Effective Christian Caregiving

By Stan E. DeKoven, Ph. D

From Hurt to Healed
Effective Christian Caregiving
By Stan E. DeKoven

ISBN 978-1-61529-028-4

Published by:

VISION PUBLISHING
RAMONA, CA 92065
1-800-9-VISION

WWW.VISIONPUBLISHINGSERVICES.COM

All scripture references are taken from the New American Standard Version of the bible unless otherwise noted.
This book was printed in the United States of America.

Table of Contents

INTRODUCTION

The need for care and caregiving of Christians and non-Christians alike is an art form requiring skills and a heart of compassion. The needs of human beings are complex, and the solutions to these complex problems require knowledge, insight, and understanding.

The majority of home fellowship leaders, elders, deacons, and even pastors often avoid the important pastoral function of caregiving. Though most believers do not require long-term care, all need understanding, empathy, warmth, respect, and discipleship, which require knowledge of the kinds of problems people generally face and how to address them with wisdom.

In this booklet, the key elements of caregiving for lay leaders are presented with a focus on the biblical, while minimizing the theoretical. A practical solution is presented along with processes to assist in uncovering reasons for maladaptive or dysfunctional behavior and guidance to help someone overcome problems and move forward in their Christian walk.

The question for most leaders is not if caregiving will be done, but will we be effective in the process and do no harm to those God has placed in our charge. I hope this book will help the reader to be used by God as a minister of grace and mercy for the precious souls in need of Christian care.

Stan DeKoven, Ph.D.

CHAPTER 1

HISTORICAL GUIDE TO PASTORAL CAREGIVING

Five Primary Pastoral Functions[1]

Howard Clinebell (1990) has categorized five pastoral functions that have existed since the beginning of the first century church. These include:

1. **Healing**: wholeness or completeness in one's life. One of the primary pastoral functions is to bring about healing into the lives of the people the pastor ministers to.

2. **Sustaining**: the ability to assist people to handle the difficult times in their lives. These include the crises of life that are developmentally oriented or situationally determined.

3. **Guiding**: removing confusion from people and giving them a set of beliefs and standards they can live by and trust.

4. **Reconciling**: the reestablishing of relationships that have been broken, both with the Lord and with one another.

5. **Nurturing**: helping people to sense the security and affirmation of being loved within the Body of Christ.

From the beginning, pastors have attempted to meet the needs of people through the activities of preaching, teaching, and caregiving. In reality, this places a tremendous burden on the Man

---

[1] **An expanded version of this can be found in the author's book, On Belay: Introduction to Christian Care Giving.**

or Woman of God. Why would that be? Historically the church has had an average of 70 people. In the age of the mega church, and with the tremendous needs of modern society, it is very difficult for one pastor to meet all of the needs that are present in the people's lives.

Therefore, it is essential that there be a trained laity to be able to minister alongside the local pastor to ensure that the needs of the people are met. One of the primary areas essential in helping people grow in the things of the Lord is discipleship caregiving. With effectual trained lay leaders, more of God's walking wounded can become the people that God wants them to be.

WHAT IS CHRISTIAN CARE GIVING?

Christian caregiving is an adjunct to pastoral ministry, which focuses on helping someone with personal challenges and problems, and to solve them as a part of ongoing care and discipleship. This type of care is not like psychotherapy, which requires a trained professional, and sometimes **5 years or 50,000 dollars, whichever comes first, but is short term and focused care, primarily during a crisis, or to solve an immediate problem requiring biblical wisdom and common sense.**

ASSUMPTIONS OF BIBLICAL CARE GIVING

Christian caregiving is based on the assumption that to give healthy care to a new convert or struggling saint requires an **understanding of human behavior consistent with the Christian world view and the teaching of God's word.**

Listed below are some of the basic assumptions that are the basis for Christian caregiving.

1. **Man was created perfect and whole in the very image of a personal Divine Creator and** therefore **was innately**

good, although predisposed towards maladjustment. Original sin is passed on from generation to generation, not specifically as a genetic code, but unintentionally and clearly through our parents.

2. Men and women are **tripartite beings:** they are body, soul and spirit. Optimum health can only occur when a balance is obtained in all three areas of life. An intimate relationship with the Lord is essential for complete happiness, as well as attaining the knowledge that heaven is the ultimate home of the Christian.

3. Every individual has an **innate potential to be fulfilled**. God has a wonderful plan for each person's life. Disease may occur on any of the three levels (body, soul or spirit) of our lives. All three areas must be taken into account when dealing with an individual's life. Jesus was sent to be the provision for man so that mankind could be redeemed and reconciled into a right relationship with God. Once that regeneration occurs, man is able to again walk in fellowship with God and to resume his original mission in life (John 3:15-17; Rom. 5:15-21; I Cor. 5:7).

4. This redemption, reconciliation and regeneration provided by Christ's death on the cross must be personally received and experienced by each individual in order to acquire the benefits from it (John 3: 1-15; Rom. 10: 9-17).

5. Each person's experience is a "new birth" of God's life and essence within them which may take place in a crisis situation, or gradually as one grows spiritually in their personal faith and relationship with Christ.

6. Regardless of how one's life in Christ has begun, spiritual growth is moving toward spiritual maturity through a

process of putting off the old man and putting on the new man (Eph.4:15-24; Rom. 6:11-23).

FURTHER CONCEPTS OF MAN

Man is unique. Mankind is by far the most superior creature in the world. He is rational and is a spiritual being. (Psalms 8:5; John 3:16; and Heb. 2:9).

Mankind is sinful. As previously stated, it is known that men have fallen short of God's glory and have missed the mark (Gen. 3:6; Psa. 53:3; 94:11; Rom. 3:10; I John 1:8). Because of the separation of mankind from God, men are condemned and need a savior (John 3:17-19; Rom. 5:12).

Finally, **men are free to choose**. God created man with the ability to make free choices. God did not want mankind to love Him out of obligation, but he desired to receive love by choice. Man must choose to follow Him and to follow the biblical principles of life (John 8:36; Rom. 6:7, 12; Gal. 5:1).

WINDOWS OF TRUTH

In the Garden of Eden, there were two trees specifically talked about: the tree of life and the tree of the knowledge of good and evil. Revelation, knowledge about Christ, His plan and purpose for man, salvation, etc., are received from the tree of life. Jesus is the Way, the Truth, and the Life. Therefore Christ and His Word are the truth, our absolute authority flowing from God's throne through the tree of life revealed to us through Christ and his word.

Psychological truth, other than that which is revealed in God's Word, must come from the tree of knowledge. Not all that comes from this tree is evil, as many writers might suggest, but some natural truth is good and usable in our daily lives. The key is to be able to ferret out the jewels from the junk: the good knowledge from that which is evil.

All of us see things slightly differently. The report given by different people of the same event can be vastly different. You will see why more clearly in the section on communication.

Men and women throughout history have seen and recorded events, made hypotheses and conclusions, some of which have withstood the tests of time (for example the law of gravity), others have been modified when new knowledge was uncovered (for example the theory that the sun revolved around the earth).

The key understanding for us is that the truth is what we seek for ourselves and others, the source of all truth is God, and biblical truth is always superior to natural or scientific truth. Helping people find their way, know the Truth and live the life of Christ in the world is our goal.

THE PROCESS OF INTEGRATION

Therefore, **what makes Christian caregiving unique is the fact that the Bible is the final authority and standard of behavior for all.** All schools of thought in psychotherapy have a foundation and/or frame of reference from which they operate. The Word of God is the foundation for Christian caregivers. They accept that the Bible is the authentic guide and authority for their lives. It provides the Christian with that which is needed to enable them to fulfill the historical goal of pastoral care as discussed earlier. The **Christian caregiver uses both biblical insights and balanced understanding of human behavior, knowing that the** Bible is the final authority of belief and aids the Christian in understanding the deepest needs of mankind.

Further, the Christian caregiver must depend on the **power of the Holy Spirit** to see lives changed. They not only depend on their own will power, insight or wisdom for assisting people in making changes in their lives, but they deeply believe in the enabling, indwelling power of the Holy Spirit to bring about change.

Christian caregiving offers a way for people to deal with the hurts and traumas of their past. This is a vitally important part of the caregiving ministry in that many of the deepest needs of mankind are due to traumatic past experiences yet unresolved. In Philippians 3:13-14 can be seen the importance Paul places on letting go of things of the past. Paul says,

> "Brothers, I do not consider myself yet to have taken hold of it. But one thing I do: forgetting what is behind and straining toward what is ahead, I press on toward the goal to win the prize for which God has called me heavenward in Christ Jesus."

A wise caregiver understands their function in assisting people to press toward the goal and, as the Holy Spirit reveals negative areas of an individual's life (that is the job of the Holy Spirit, not just a probing and nosy caregiver), God will bring healing to individuals' lives.

A part of every caregiver's need is to **live daily in the scriptures**.

> "Trust in the Lord with all your heart and lean not on your own understanding; in all your ways acknowledge Him, and He will make your paths straight" (Proverbs 3:5-6).

Christian caregivers need to have direction from the Holy Spirit to assist them in the guiding process of people to whom they have the privilege of ministering.

Christian caregivers deal with the whole man, believing God through Jesus Christ and His atonement, brings total healing

for the total man: spirit, soul and body; all of which are integrated and need to be brought into an integrated balance.

The Christian caregiving process, whether done in an individual setting, a group setting, or even from a teaching point of view; is designed to assist people in understanding the Biblical concepts of growth and change. It also helps them to effectively apply these principles in daily life.

When an individual comes to know Christ as his or her Savior, it is the **spirit** of man that comes to life: they are born again. It is important to remember, however, the soul of man is not regenerated at that time. The spirit of man communicates with the Lord (John 4:23) and has perception and insight that is separate from mental reasoning and functioning. **The soul of man** (the mind, the will and the emotions) must be regenerated through the process known as **progressive sanctification,** renewing the mind (Rom. 12:1,2) or the putting off of the old man and the putting on of the new man as described in Ephesians, chapter 4.

CAREGIVING AND THE NEED

In Ephesians 4:16 Paul says.

> "...from who the whole body being fitted together by that which every joint supplies according to the proper working of each individual part causes the growth of the body for the building up of itself in love" (NAS).

Caregiving ministry is **discipleship.** The Holy Spirit's role as comforter and paraclete or caregiver is to help Christians conform to the image of Christ. In II Corinthians, chapter 1 the Apostle Paul states that Christians are all to be involved in the comforting or caregiving ministry. Christians are to come alongside one another and give care and assistance. Caregiving can be both a discipleship and healing ministry within the Body of Christ.

Also, Christians need to learn to be able to **comfort** those who are hurting, and to bring **correction** to those not living according to God's principles. In Galatians, chapter 6, the Christian is instructed to **bear** one another's burdens, to **nurture** others and to bring **edification** or encouragement to those in the body of Christ.

WHO CAN GIVE CARE?

While everyone can give care and encouragement, not everyone is an effective caregiver. This is one problem often seen in pastoral ministry. **Most pastors are not specifically trained in giving counsel, yet all of them will counsel.** The only real question is, will they counsel effectively and with the power of God? Or will they do so impotently and ineffectively? The qualifications of someone involved in Christian caregiving should be somewhat obvious, but for purposes of clarity they are listed here:

1. Caregivers need to be people who have a personal and vibrant relationship with the Lord Jesus Christ.
2. Caregivers should be under the authority of a local church.
3. It is important that caregivers have a proper attitude of heart. They must have a heart and mind of a servant leader.
4. Wisdom is needed, wisdom that comes from God.
5. Knowledge must be added to all of the above requirements. The caregiver needs information that will provide the training needed in the area of ministry.
6. Caregivers cannot minister above their level of wholeness.

WHAT IS THE OVERALL GOAL OF CAREGIVING?

There are many goals of caregiving. The first it is to **give hope**. In I Corinthians 13 it says three things abide or continue: faith, hope and love. Many people have faith, but when results are not seen, or change does not happen overnight, they develop a sense of hopelessness. Jesus came to give hope, both eternal hope as well as hope for the present. Part of the ministry of Christian caregiving is to offer hope to people.

Also, as previously mentioned, it gives **encouragement** in life. Caregiving helps people deal with problem areas of life such as worry, anxiety, guilt, depression, anger, and issues of the flesh.

Caregiving will also **assist people to grow** in the things of God and to develop more spiritual awareness of who they are in Christ and what the Lord's expectations for them are. People of proven character in all areas of life are needed as examples to others.

AREAS OF LIFE AFFECTED BY CAREGIVING

Men are created as **Tri-partite beings**. They are made up of three primary components, inseparable and intertwined. The three parts are: spirit, soul and body. **It can be noted that the primary problems "born again" people have in their lives are not in the area of their spirit, but are primarily in the areas of soul and body.**

What a person thinks about himself and others will determine much of whom he is and what he is like in the world. If the thought life is primarily negative, then most of the feeling and behavior will be negative also. In Phil. 4:8 Paul suggests that

> "Finally brethren, whatever is true, whatever is honorable, whatever is right, whatever is pure, whatever is lovely, whatever is of good repute, if there is excellence and anything worthy of praise, **let your mind dwell on these things.**"

The mind must be renewed and brought into a right relationship with the Word of God in order to become whole and complete. Romans 1:28 says,

15

"And just as they did not see fit to acknowledge God any longer, God gave them over to a depraved (or reprobate) mind to do those things that are not proper."

If men do not follow after the things of God, even though they may be born again, they could become reprobate or depraved. Man's thinking process could become so distorted or delusional he would be unable to see the truth. This distorted or delusional thinking may be why some people, even though they are born again and perhaps even filled with the Holy Spirit, continue to do and make the same mistakes over and over again: mistakes that are clearly against the will of God for their lives.

Learning to renew the mind is a must if Christians are to function fully within the Body of Christ. A part of the caregiving ministry is to **bring truth in areas where lies had a foothold.** In the caregiving process, it is inherent that an individual be helped to **become aware of their self talk** and especially of the negative thoughts they feed themselves on a daily basis. Once aware of those negative thoughts, using the Word of God, and in some cases natural logic, they can be assisted in overcoming the erroneous information or disbelief and lies they have believed to be true.

Thoughts + Actions = Behavior

Another important step in eliminating negative thoughts for the Christian is to affiliate with or develop relationships with people who are more positive in nature. Negativity attracts negativity. There is an old adage that says, "Misery loves company." Miserable people tend to find other people who commiserate with them. If one finds all they attract is negative people, perhaps it is because of their own negativity.

The Word of God stresses the need for **obedience to the Word**. Helping people come into compliance with the word of God is a key to growth and happiness.

WHY CHRISTIANS HAVE EMOTIONAL PROBLEMS

There are many reasons why Christians are subject to the same maladies as non-Christians. The Bible does say that the rain falls on the just and the unjust alike (Matthew 5:45). In the world, there is tribulation and trouble. Jesus said the Christian should be of good cheer for He has overcome the world (John 16:33). It is His desire that all men should also be overcomers. However, while in this body of flesh, man is still subject to the troubles and stresses of this world.

Some reasons born again people can have psychological problems include their **genetic makeup (temperament)**, their **environment**, their overall **physical health**, and of course, **stress.** Stress is known to be one of the primary causes of both psychological and physiological problems. In fact, it is estimated from 70-90% of all psychological and physical disorders are caused by an underlying inability to cope with stress.

Almost everyone is acquainted with people who suffer from depression, anxiety, phobias, and psychosomatic disorders, such as severe headaches (migraine) and other disorders of that nature. These disorders are mainly the result of the inability to cope with stress. Many problems could be avoided if people were able to live according to Biblical principles. In some cases people are unable to act on these principles because of ignorance, lack of knowledge, or a blockage in their ability to perceive and understand the meaning contained in the Scriptures.

CHAPTER II

HOW PERSONALITY DEVELOPS

Human beings were not meant to be placed in boxes or categories; they are whole people who must be seen in terms of a continuum. That is, they are in the process of becoming. This can best be seen as discussed in James 1:2-4 where it says, "my brethren, count it all joy when you fall into diverse temptations (or testings), knowing this, that the trying of your faith worketh patience. Let patience have her perfect work that you may be perfect and entire, wanting nothing."

Much of who a person is as a believer is predicated on their response to trials and temptations they experience. As Christians go through trials victoriously without falling into sin, they grow and change, becoming more and more conformed to the image of Christ. Peter declared in I Peter 1:6-7

> "wherein you greatly rejoice though now for a season if need be you are in heaviness through manifold temptations, that the trial of your faith being much more precious than fine gold that perishes, though it be tried by fire, might be found unto praise and honor and glory at the appearing of Jesus Christ."

The pressures and stresses of life can assist people to grow, to become who they are supposed to be. Each one must develop as an individual. God is constantly changing people from glory unto glory (II Cor. 3:18). This is an exciting concept, for God is changing Christians and molding them. No matter what type of personality structure a person may have, whether that personality was the product of birth or environment or both, God, by His power and grace can change anyone into what He has determined that person to be.

There are many theories of personality. None are truly a comprehensive picture of the complexity of man. Rather than focusing on the personality theories commonly accepted, a look at God's character or personality and helping people become like Jesus is our goal.

CHARACTERISTICS OF DIVINE PERSONALITY

Dr. Gary Sweetan has developed a fairly comprehensive list called the Characteristics of Divine Personality. Though there is no such thing as the perfect personality, if there were one, it would mirror the divine image of God. Listed here are many of the personality traits or characteristics that an individual would have if he/she were reflecting the divine image of God.

1. To forgive. To consciously relieve another of guilt and to restore harmony.
2. To covenant. To give promises and pledges, etc.
3. To be compassionate. To enter into another's experience in such a way that their condition becomes mine.
4. To symbolize. Not only concretely but abstractly in a creative way.
5. To be creative. To rearrange in combinations other than that which had previously existed.
6. To worship. Deliberately intended awe and respect.
7. To be self-conscious. Incompletely so, nevertheless one has the ability to hold oneself in conscious attention and to be aware of who one is.
8. To be evaluative. The use of standards to evaluate on a number of bases simultaneously, independent of one's own needs, etc.
9. To be rational. The use of logical thought patterns.
10. To hate. A selective evaluative not necessarily an emotional ability to set out to destroy or the desire to destroy.

11. To love. To deliberately act in a way that ensures the best for another.
12. Wisdom. The fear of God is the beginning of wisdom. Akin to wisdom is reverence.
13. To be responsible. Accountability in a moral sense.
14. The ability to decide. To make categories of morality.
15. The ability to know deity.
16. The ability to know Satan. Communicate, experience, interact with Satan.
17. The ability to have spiritual qualities. God transcends time and matter. It is not impossible to believe that He shared those attributes, at least partially, with man.
18. Sexuality. The spiritual, communal, personal, and physical aspect of this ability is compared to Christ and the church and the Trinity.
19. Communicability. Thoughts, feelings, hunches, intuitions, hopes, dreams, failures, successes, and fantasies can be communicated unicuely inter-humanly.
20. To govern. Intentional designation of social and legislative mores for the human is like God who consciously chooses to set rules and govern by them.
21. Dynability. The use of power and force in a consciously chosen way.
22. Sociability. The entering into the lives of other persons emotionally, spiritually, etc.
23. Cooperability. The ability to consciously cooperate or not and how much, when, and for how long.
24. Understandability. A state of awareness at the conscious and intuitive level of relationships, situations, associations, and how these relate to the past, present and future.
25. Shareability. The ability of giving of oneself materially, emotionally, intellectually or choosing to withhold those things.
26. Empathy. The ability to enter into another person's life frame and experience with him or keep him cognitively aware of the present situation.

27. Warmth. To communicate caring love to another in both specific and non-specific areas.
28. Sensitivity. Deliberately choosing to relate to a person at their level of state or experiencing reality.
29. Respect. Communicating to another person that they are valued for their own worth and personhood.
30. Peace. A term denoting creaturely wholesomeness, health, congruence, affection, to be able to communicate, emotional care, tenderness in life, non-judgmental acceptance, ability to love the sinner and hate sin.
31. Holiness. To be without flaw or sin.
32. Justice. To act toward others on the basis of righteousness. The ability to make non-determined choices.

As can be seen, to totally reflect divinity would be an impossibility. God is the only one with the perfect personality. Yet **Jesus** was the direct mirrored image of God the Father, and he, through a divine process, is **beginning to transform men into that same image by the Holy Spirit.** Man may not fully arrive at that point of perfection, but he can know that by His grace we will one day be like He is.

CHAPTER III

THE PROCESS OF CAREGIVING

Attention is now turned to some of the primary steps of caregiving and to some of the attitudes necessary to be an effective Christian **Caregiver. Caregivers who are by nature more cognitive or thinking oriented, will be more concerned about the thinking process, while those who are more feeling oriented will be more concerned about the expression of feelings. Those who are more behaviorally oriented will think more in terms of behavior.** As a caregiver however, it is important to have a balance in all areas.

Also, there are certain scriptural principles that can be used as models showing that caregivers need to be good listeners. A good listener is not one who just hears with their ears, but hears with their heart as well. This is called **listening with the third ear** or the ability to have discernment or perception as to what is going on inside of the counselee's life. One way to understand whether or not one is hearing something correctly is by getting adequate feedback.

The Christian caregiver also needs to be motivated by an attitude of love, and to develop a feeling of proper timing. The right word spoken by the right person at the right time can bring about great change and has therapeutic value (Pro. 25:11, 12). Also, as in every area of Christian caregiving, confidentiality is very important. Secrets must be kept. This can be somewhat of a dilemma if the caregiver is in the role of leadership within the local church. One thing must be clarified with the local pastor is that **communication received in the caregiving office is privileged;** that is, the individual sharing their heart has the privilege of sharing with others or not sharing with others. The caregiver does not have the right of sharing with others unless the counselee gives them permission to do so.

SEVEN STEPS TO HEALTHY CAREGIVING

The process of caregiving takes on several steps which will be briefly examined here. They include:

1. **Establish a good rapport** with the client. Empathy, warmth, respect and genuineness are of utmost importance.
2. **Explore the problems** by asking probing questions to determine possible causes of the problem presented.
3. **Discerning of causes.** Many times discernment comes from the history taking as the needs of the client are explored. Sometimes however, discernment comes from a revelation or illumination from the Lord.
4. **Repentance is a key;** the first stage of repentance is **confession.** The client must be able to confess the faults, the needs, the concerns by telling the truth about their situation and owning-up to the responsibility for the problems in their lives.
5. **Renewing of the mind** or changing the way one thinks is a part of repentance, and an ongoing process.
6. **New behaviors** are to be acted upon, or by faith the person is to try new ways of living according to Christian principles. All of the forgoing processes lead to what might be called the structuring of change. Part of the responsibility of the Christian caregiver is to assist the client in finding different options other than the ones they have been using.
7. **Evaluation is needed,** or making sure the client is being prepared for life without a mentor or discipler.

It is important that the caregiver recognizes that his role is that of a comforter and a helper. The caregiver functions in human form like the Holy Spirit. The Holy Spirit comes alongside an individual to assist the counselee in dealing with a difficult area in their life. It is of the utmost importance not to become a rescuer or a kind of Messiah. Each counselee must be responsible for their own behavior and hurt, but the caregiver is there to assist in the bearing of burdens and thus fulfilling the law of Christ (Gal.6:2).

There is always a need to understand the differences between sympathy and empathy. **Sympathy is an expression of sorrow for someone's grief.** Empathy, however, is the capacity for participating with another person in the feeling of grief (or any other emotion for that matter). **Empathy is to walk with someone.** It is a relationship building skill.

In Summation:

Herewith are some additional thoughts that can assist the caregiver to become more effective in this helping ministry:

Attend carefully to the needs of the client, through the listening process. Listen to the primary core issues of the individual's heart. Hear the cry of the heart, not just the words that are said.

The caregiver should not do most of the talking. A good rule of thumb is the caregiver should not talk more than one third of the time. The counselee needs to discover some of their own answers as they search the Word and as they talk through the problems in their lives.

Remember, it is their life, and they are ultimately responsible for their problems. You are not the healer, God is.

CAREGIVING GOALS

What then is the overall goal of caregiving? That is, what is the caregiver attempting to do in the caregiving ministry? The Apostle Paul in Colossians wrote that his interaction with people was always designed to promote Christian maturity. This is one way the caregiving process may be defined. **In Biblical or Christian caregiving a major strategy is the promotion of both spiritual and psychological growth and maturity.** Maturity involves two primary elements. First is **immediate obedience** in specific situations. Secondly, there is the need to see **long range character growth** or change. The Apostle Paul indicated the need to become conformed to the image of Christ. That "conforming" is a process and not an event and, although it begins at the moment one is born again, it is not complete until the time the Christian is glorified. The goal of Christian caregiving is to promote Christian maturity and to help people enter into a richer experience of worship and effective service for the Lord. In broad terms, Christian maturity is developed by dealing with any immediate problem in a manner consistent with Scripture and by developing an inward character which conforms to the character or image of Christ.

CAREGIVING APPROACH

Following is a summary of the four most valuable suggestions to be made in helping the caregiver offer balanced and effective care:

1. Have a genuine care about people.
2. Develop what is called an indirect-direct approach to caregiving in which the clients are assisted in coming to their own conclusions about the direction God wishes them to take.
3. Help the clients formulate a specific plan of action in view of their problem(s).
4. Assist clients in making the right decisions that will bring about change. It is the ministry of the Holy Spirit to bring people into all truth.

CHAPTER IV

PROBLEMS THAT CAN OCCUR IN CAREGIVING

Caregiving is a process and many problems are inherent in the process. Some of the problems include:

1. **Not every client is going to tell the truth about their whole story** or, at best, they will distort the reality of situations because they are looking at the situation through their own eyes.
2. Another major problem that can occur has to do with the an individual and how they got to be the way they are is known (what social dynamic or family dynamics have led to the present situation) then it may not be possible to come to a proper conclusion and give adequate counsel. This lack of sufficient information has happened many times to marriage and family caregivers. **It is better to err to the side of getting too much information than not enough.**
3. At times clients will lack **the motivation for change**. They may be coming to caregiving because they have been pressured by a spouse who has said, "If you don't change, I'll divorce you." Part of the responsibility of the caregiver is to motivate the clients by presenting the Word of God and presenting how Jesus wants them to grow in His grace and knowledge.
4. Another problem in caregiving can occur because of the **authority vested in the caregiver**. A Christian leader does operate under the authority or the mantle of the Holy Spirit, as a priest would have, or a wise man in the Old Testament. This authority **should only be used for the benefit of others.**
5. Caregiving ministry deals to a great extent with heightened and often intense **emotions.** Emotions are by nature

unstable and illogical, and should not be expected to be otherwise. The goal is to assist the person to process through their feelings so as to understand that their **thought life is what triggers those emotions. They must learn to renew their minds so they can control the emotions**

A short summary of caregiving guidelines may be helpful before moving to the next section of this book on specific problems to address in caregiving ministry.

1. Cooperation with the Holy Spirit is imperative.
2. Confidentiality is essential.
3. Timing is very important.
4. Good listening skills must be developed.
5. The caregiver should be aware of any previous caregiving.
6. The Word of God is an indispensable tool in caregiving.
7. The leader should take every opportunity to help the client build a healthy response toward God.

Of course, to properly care for someone begins with a good understanding of the problem, which is often referred to as assessment.

LEVELS OF ASSESSMENT

Assessment can occur on **three different levels**.

1. The first is a **peer caregiving** level in which the caregiver uses empathy, warmth, and respect to show understanding to an individual. The first level of assessment is nothing more than an interview where probing questions are asked to assist the client in talking about what is happening in their life or what is causing them problems. During this level, which may take from one to three hours, listening with great understanding and empathy is essential.

2. A slightly more advanced level of assessment would be a **clinical pastoral** level. At this level, the pastoral caregiver may give a minor **psychological test** or may go into greater depths in regard to the client's history with probing questions. At this level the caregiver may even seek, in an ethical manner, input from the outside such as from another pastor, teacher, physician or other persons who may have had some influence in the client's life.

3. The **advanced professional** level deals with **significant psychological testing and assessment**.

The bottom line is **if a caregiver is to function effectively, he must be able to define what the problem is within an individual's life.**

SUMMARY OF STEPS USEFUL IN DETERMINING THE NEEDS OF A CLIENT

The caregiver needs certain criteria by which to reach conclusions concerning the counselee and his/her personality trends, needs, and deficits. Some of the criteria are listed as follows:

1. **Make notes** of the circumstances of the referral and the presenting problem.
2. **Write a simple statement** of who the counselee is and a brief statement, as much as possible in the client's own words, of what he/she understands the problem to be. Such questions as the following are helpful:
   a. "How long have you had this problem?"
   b. "When did the problem first begin?
   c. "How long have the episodes lasted?"
   d. "What has helped you in the past?
   e. "Have you previously sought caregiving help?"
   f. "Are you taking any medication? What kind?

g. "What event has recently precipitated the problem?"
3. **Get a past history.** What has happened in the past may play a very important role in the present problem. The past is often still present with each client. People often repeat patterns from the past.

Remember, one bit of information does not tell the whole story. That is why **much information must be gathered** and then, after carefully reviewing it and through times of prayer and seeking guidance from the Lord, the whole picture of the client's needs comes together. Only after gathering as much information as possible, should you begin the process of assisting with problem solving with the client.

THE IMPORTANCE OF COMMUNICATION

Communication is the sending and receiving of a message from one person to another sent in such a way so that it is clearly understood by both parties. True communication only occurs when there is a sense of communion or understanding between two or more parties. There are three types of communication, verbal, written and non-verbal that may be used in Christian caregiving. In each form of communication there are advantages and disadvantages as noted in the following:

In the **verbal** form it is fairly easy to hear what an individual is saying and to make sense of it. The English language however, is filled with words that have double and sometimes triple meanings to them. For example, the word love can be used for anything from hot dogs to a deep relationship; one of the rudimentary functions of communications is to ensure that **what is being heard is what the other person meant to say.**

In the **written** form it is normally easier to understand what the individual is trying to say. The problem with the written form of communication is that it is **difficult to ask for further**

information. It is sometimes necessary to "read into" what has been written.

Non-verbal communication, or as it is sometimes called "body language," states that there are **certain statements that could be made by gestures that are fairly clear to most people,** especially in the English speaking world. However, in many other forms of body language it is difficult to understand the true meaning. As noted earlier, sometimes people cross their arms because they are more comfortable that way.

For those involved in Christian caregiving it is important to be aware of the usage of all three types of communication. At times the first contact a caregiver will have with a client will be on the telephone or in a personal contact. Some form of communication is going on at all times.

SIMPLE MODEL OF COMMUNICATION

The simple communication process starts with a message that a person wants to communicate. When the individual sends the message, whether it is in verbal, written or non-verbal form; it first passes through the individual person's **in-coder.** The in-coder is made up of their perceptions, beliefs, history and mood for **that day.** It goes through the in-coder and in that in-coder there is a certain amount of noise or distortion that will occur in the message. Although a person may think that he is communicating clearly, what is being received by the hearer may not be so clear.

The person receiving the message then must decode the meaning. They **de-code** as their perceptual grid **attempts to determine what was meant by the sender**. Further difficulty is encountered if the message comes from more than one type of communication. For example, if someone were to say, "I really love you," with their fists clenched and the veins in their neck popping out, there are two distinctly different messages being sent. It therefore becomes paramount for the individual to find out what meaning was really behind the message being sent. The message must be "decoded" so full understanding can occur. Because of man's imperfection and the fact he does not have "all understanding," certain portions of the message and interpretation will be missed. Noises and disturbances in the receiver's decoder may interfere with clear understanding.

Asking for feedback is vitally important. Feedback is nothing more than asking whether or not the message was received correctly. Feedback may come in the form of a statement such as, "What I hear you saying is", or "I think what you meant was this. Did I hear you correctly?" Feedback is one way of making sure of clarity of information. Going through the process of feedback is not necessary in every type of communication or the communication process would be incredibly laborious. However, when first meeting a client or during the first few sessions of caregiving, the feedback technique might be used rather frequently until the caregiver feels he knows the client well enough to be sure that they are hearing the client correctly.

HINDRANCES TO GOOD COMMUNICATION -- NOISE

It is an accepted fact that people have trouble communicating with one another. **Probably the foremost reason for the lack of good communication is that everyone has certain prejudices.** Each person views the world from a different perspective. Secondly, each individual, even though they many share the same prejudice, might have a slightly different bias in relationship to that prejudice. Thirdly, and most important in the caregiving process, is the history of the individual client. That is, many are filled with anger, fears or anxiety, or perhaps have been victimized at one time or another in their past. This has tainted their perception of themselves, their perception of others, male, female relationships, etc. These perceptions of self or self-concept are developed over time and are not easily overcome, which is why the communication process in caregiving is so vitally important. The skilled Christian must learn to communicate effectively and clearly, and as mentioned before, the first stage is to become an excellent listener.

SOME RULES FOR EFFECTIVE COMMUNICATION

1. One must always be aware of any discrepancies between verbal and non-verbal communication. Note taking and careful listening are imperative.

2. Communication needs to be two way and open ended. Open ended can be illustrated by the following questions:

    "Do you like spaghetti?"
    (*Closed ended can be answered with either yes or no.*)

    "What is your favorite kind of food?"
    (*Open ended cannot be answered with yes or no.*)

3. Respect the uniqueness of others.

4. Be open to the Holy Spirit. He is the guide.

5. Learn to listen with what has been called the third ear.

6. Set aside preconceived beliefs about the client and about caregiving.

7. Avoid preconceived notions about the way people are supposed to talk. Occasionally a client may use very colorful or explicit language. It is important not to judge them but to assist them in getting to a place where they can communicate effectively without using irreverent slang.

8. Remember that **communication is irreversible** (See Proverbs 13:3 and 17:4). Once something has been said it is not possible to unsay it. It is therefore important to use great care in what is said to the client so that it is always therapeutic and never harmful.

CHAPTER V

PROBLEMS AND CAREGIVING

Introduction

Generally, men and women, young people, couples or children are in the caregiving office due to problems that have become beyond their ability to cope with. The problems people face are varied and at times immense, and they are seeking caregiving for answers or alleviation of suffering. Therefore, it is important that the Christian leader know as much as possible about the various problems experienced by those who come in for caregiving.

ANXIETY

Psychologists have stated that anxiety is one of the most urgent problems of the day. Anxiety is an inner feeling of apprehension, uneasiness, concern, or worry that is accompanied by a heightened physical arousal. Another way of describing anxiety is that it is the **psychological feeling of pain.** It is an emotional sense of dread that creates great problems for much of society.

There are four primary types of anxiety:
1. **ACUTE ANXIETY.** Acute anxiety comes on quickly and with high intensity and has a short duration. Some of the symptoms include: shortness of breath, thickening of the tongue, a sense that one is going to pass out or die, a rapid heartbeat or palpitations, and beads of perspiration on the brow. In modern day language this is referred to as a **"panic attack"** or "**panic disorder**".

2. **CHRONIC ANXIETY.** Chronic anxiety is a **persistent, long lasting, lower intensity anxiety or fear.** People will worry most all of the time regarding a variety of situations.

3. **NORMAL ANXIETY.** Normal anxiety has to do with the experience of **fear when faced with a real situation or threat of danger**. God created man with an internalized, biological arousal system which says, "Danger! Run!" If a person wants to run every time they see a picture of a lion, they are experiencing anxiety on the anxiety attack or chronic anxiety level. However, if an individual opens his front door and comes face to face with a real roaring lion and experiences anxiety it is better called "common sense," or normal anxiety.

4. **OBSESSIVE COMPULSIVE ANXIETY.** Obsessive compulsive anxiety is called neurotic anxiety. In modern terminology this level of anxiety is called an excessive or compulsive anxiety state or a sense of exaggerated fear and helplessness. It is usually caused by irrational belief systems and unconscious inner conflict.

There are many causes of anxiety, most of which begin early in childhood. Simply stated, there are threats that come against everyone at one time or another. Threats that may be either physical or psychological in nature -- threats come in different forms. Some threats can affect one's sense of self worth. Some threats come from some form of conflict which can also take on different forms, such as not getting one's basic needs met, the fear of failure, the fear of success, fear of rejection, loneliness, sickness, death, etc. Finally, there can be an anxiety that comes from unmet needs. These unmet needs might include the need to survive, the need for a feeling of significance in the world, the need to reach certain goals, the need for a sense of purpose and identity. The effects of anxiety can include anything from mild physical and psychological reactions to severe breakdown in bodily functions, often called psychosomatic illness.

TREATMENT FOR ANXIETY

The type and duration of anxiety a person is experiencing determines the type of treatment. In some cases **medication** can be helpful. These cases should be referred to a psychiatrist or an internal medicine specialist who could monitor medication. Medication at best should be for short term relief. It rarely constitutes a cure. Normally, to see someone overcome anxiety it takes a change in the thinking process as well as an understanding of the Word of God in regard to anxiety. It is important to help people understand what the Word of God says. God promises a rest for his people... In Hebrews the writer speaks of our entering into that rest. There is a labor -- a birthing process -- in the new birth that brings people into the rest as the people of God. When the Christian begins to understand who God is and who they are in Christ they can begin to understand the peace that passes all understanding. God promised that peace, yet many people do not understand what that feeling would be like. There are three primary causes for the problem. 1) people are so busy rushing around **seeking things** they never experience that rest, 2) people do not remember their lives are to be spent living for God and for others, 3) God created man to worship. Worship of God creates in itself a sense of calm and peace and can help rescue individuals from the world of stress and anxiety.

In the book of Philippians it talks about not perpetually worrying about one thing after another, but instead finding that place of peace which only God can provide. The Christian caregiver can often model that peace by **demonstrating how to relax and rest in the presence of the Lord.** Relaxation techniques can be taught. The caregiver can teach physical ways of anxiety reduction such as physical exercise.

Anxiety is a major problem in the world. Christian caregivers have the answers to the needs of people suffering from anxiety. The client can be brought to freedom through a relationship with Jesus

Christ, because **Jesus can break the power of canceled sin and set the prisoner free.**

SUBSTANCE ABUSE

Alcohol has been used for a number of purposes, including medicinal, over the centuries. Its abuse, as well as the abuse of other controlled substances, causes tremendous problems throughout the world. Literally millions of dollars are spent each year on the consumption of alcohol as well as the treatment of alcoholism and other forms of substance abuse.

Some of the primary causes for the abuse of any substance include the following:
1. The level of stress within the individual's life.
2. Low self-esteem.
3. Peer pressure.
4. A spiritual vacuum.

1. The **level of stress** within Western culture has become immense. When people are under severe stress they will look for ways to escape the stress they experience. Demonstrated through the media and the observation of one's family (in many cases) the use of a substance to deaden the pain of one's daily existence is frequently modeled. Because of that modeling process, it becomes an option for people to use a substance to relieve stress or anxiety.
2. **Self-image** has to do with how a person thinks about himself/herself, about his intellectual ability, physical characteristics, personality, and talents. The characteristics of a poor self-image can be described as follows:
   a. One who finds it difficult to accept compliments from others.
   b. An individual who has trouble developing close relationships.

c. A person who puts himself down on a regular basis. One who takes constructive criticism personally and gets depressed or angry about it.
d. A person who believes inaccurate criticism to be true and takes it to heart.
e. One who holds on to past failures and unconsciously punishes himself/herself for them.

Some Characteristics of a Good Self-image
1. A person who enjoys their abilities and seeks to cultivate or increase them.
2. A person who is able to see another person's poor self-image and assist them where possible.
3. A person who makes unique contributions to others.
4. A person who is able to accept compliments.
5. A person who enjoys close personal friendships.
6. A person who can take criticism and use it for their own improvement.

A person lacking a positive, godly, self-image may turn to substances to deal with life's uncertainties and bolster their sense of worth.

3. Much of substance abuse begins during the teen years. Young people are looking for acceptance and seek a peer group they can belong too. The pressure placed on them by their peers, directly or indirectly, can influence their decision to use a substance or not.

4. There is an incredible **spiritual vacuum** in the world today. The **fundamental values** of many Western nations is built on the philosophy of "Eat, drink and be merry for tomorrow we die." Therefore, in the midst of a spiritual vacuum, people will find all kinds of ways to meet what are essentially emotional and spiritual needs. They can include anything from sexual behavior, which can lead to sexual addiction, and substance abuse, to seeking for power, money and prestige, etc. **The biggest need of man today**

is that the spiritual vacuum be filled. This can only be done through a relationship with Jesus Christ.

What should the attitude of the church be toward people who have become addicted to a substance? First of all, alcohol and drug abuse, sexual addiction, and any other type of addictive process do not begin as a disease but ends that way. To condemn or criticize the one who is now in the diseased state will never bring about healing and redemption. **The attitude of the church needs to be the same attitude Jesus had toward those who were caught or stuck in repetitive sin.**

It is important to recognize that most substance abusers have a significant amount of denial in regard to their problem. That is, they reject the thought they have a problem themselves. Almost everyone has talked to people who have abused substances and heard them say, "Oh, I can quit any time I want to. I don't really have a problem with this. I couldn't be an alcoholic (or drug abuser)." **Denial is a very powerful block that keeps substance abusers from receiving the help they need.**

There are several stages of denial. The following are two of the most common:
1. The blaming stage. The individual will blame anyone in their sphere of influence as the reason they abuse a substance to keep themselves from having to face personal responsibility.
2. Rationalization. Individuals will tend to rationalize the use of the substance.

Denial is a form of an unconscious suppression of a personal responsibility for certain problematic behavior. Most alcoholics and drug abusers have a tremendous sense of guilt and shame about their behavior. They recognize how it has negatively affected their families and work environment. Therefore, **it is painful for them to face their responsibility which can lead to**

emotional and physical isolation and keep them from seeking the help they need.

It must be recognized that all of the above symptoms are indeed symptoms of alcoholism or drug abuse and **represent a disease state.** These symptoms are caused by the destructive forces within the individual's own body and by the warping of the thinking process that occurs through substance abuse. Therefore, the **process of healing** must come from three primary areas. These areas are to be found in Ephesians chapter 4 and are summarized as follows:

1. **Lay off the old self.** The individual must stop doing what they are doing, whether it is drinking, abusing drugs, sexual behavior, or something else. They must stop. Stopping harmful behavior is the first step towards getting clean from the abuse itself (Eph. 4:22).

2. **Renewal of the mind.** The renewal of the mind is probably more important than step one. Most alcoholics, drug abusers, sex addicts, etc. have guilt, anxiety, and shame which leads to self-punishment and then self-reward, creating a complete addictive cycle (Eph. 4:23).

3. **Put on the New Self.** The most difficult part of any major change, especially with substance abuse, is to begin to act by faith according to God's Word. The object is not to get people to "fake it" until they "make it," but they must "faith it" until they "make it." They must learn to act as though they were all that God created them to be (Eph. 4:24).

Millions of men and women, Christian and Non-Christian alike, have benefited greatly from the work of Alcoholic Anonymous or other Recovery programs utilizing the Twelve Steps program. This model of self-help recovery can be easily interpreted into a biblical context and used effectively in the local church.

FAMILY PROBLEMS

Families are living under more stress today than ever before in the history of the world. Radio and television continually point out the immense breakdown of the family. Families are in need of help today, and caregivers must be armed with knowledge of the challenges facing family life.

A working definition of family is: **two or more persons who are related by blood, marriage, or adoption and who are living under the same roof.** In dealing with the family, it is understood that both the immediate family and the extended family (grandparents, uncles, aunts, in-laws, etc.) are all considered as part of the family system. Historically, the primary function of the family has been to do the following:

1. **For reproduction.** This includes the regulation of sex and children and to provide the limits of sexual behavior and childbearing.

2. **Socialization.** In the family the children are taught and trained to live according to societal rules.

3. **Companionship.** The primary social relationships that members of a family have are in terms of: family, love, intimacy and are to occur within the family structure.

It is important to understand that the **family is a system**. No one member is an island unto himself. Each member of the family is affected by the others in the family. If one member of the family begins to make a change of any type it will affect every other individual in that family.

Just a few of the needs that must be met within the family of origin are:

1. **Survival needs.** This includes food, clothing, shelter and a sense of security.

2. **Emotional and physical needs.** These needs are the essentials for growth.

3. **Formation of life goals.** To assist in the task that each individual has to reach his goals and aims in life.

The family itself has a role of responsibility for the maintenance of everybody within the family system, including the maintenance of health and safety of the family in general. Considering these factors, it is easy to see what a difficult responsibility it is for the family to meet all of those needs.

The family is a system. That is, each member responds to the others within the family. Families can be categorized as either **functional** or **dysfunctional** depending upon how well they are able to meet the needs of the members within the system.

Every family has its problems. The question is not whether a family has problems or not, but whether they have the skill to resolve their problems in a functional manner so that each individual member can grow to a place of maturity in their own life.

DYSFUNCTIONAL PATTERNS OF COMMUNICATION

Four patterns of communication in dysfunctional families often observed are:[2]

1. **Placating** -- The placator is always trying to please, always apologizing, never disagrees. He or she is a "yes man." He is always trying to get other people to approve of him. He thinks his worth is nothing and thinks he's lucky if anyone talks to him. He agrees with any criticism made about him and blames himself if anything goes wrong.

2. **Blamer** -- this is the fault-finder, the dictator, the boss. He acts superior. He cuts everyone and everything down. He throws his weight around and doesn't wait for people to answer his questions. His voice is loud and shrill.

3. **Computer** -- The computer is ultra reasonable, very correct with no semblance of any demonstrative feeling. His voice is calm, cool and collected. Compare this to a computer. His voice is monotone, and he uses the longest words possible to sound intelligent. The body and limbs are motionless and stiff. He tries to say the right words, show no feeling and doesn't react. Inside he feels very vulnerable.

4. **Distractor** -- He does or says nothing relevant to what anyone else is saying or doing. He never makes a response to the point. The voice is singsong, going up and down without reason. His arms, legs, body and mouth are busily moving. Questions are ignored and he comes back with new questions on a different subject. His inside feelings are that nobody cares; there is no place for me.

---

[2] "From the work of Virginia Satir".

In highly dysfunctional families, you will often see one or more of these communication patterns in action. Describing them and uncovering them is a key to helping the family change.

One highly effective method for helping families face their problems has been developed by writer and caregiver Jay Haley. He calls it Problem-solving Therapy, which emphasizes obtaining a clear statement of the problem and an accurate picture of the interactional sequence maintaining the problem. Goals are then set with the family, and the caregiver sets up a series of interventions that meet the goals by eliminating the problem and changing the sequence of interaction. The first interview has four stages:

1. **The social stage** -- the family is welcomed and made comfortable.

2. **The statement of the problem stage** -- each family member is asked for their view of the problem.

3. **The Interaction stage** -- the caregiver asks the family to talk with one another.

4. **The goal-setting stage** -- the family is asked to specify the changes sought from therapy.

Diagnosis is developed from studying the relationship between the symptoms or presenting problems and the repetitive sequence observed in the family.

Once the problem is defined, the caregiver formulates the treatment strategy consisting of a series of directives. Directives are usually tasks to be accomplished between visits.

Deviant behavior can be viewed in the context of the family system. The family is the manufacturer of negative behavior.

In defining deviant or wrong behavior, the definition would differ according to each family's rules and traditions.

CHILDREN AND ADOLESCENCE

Children are a great challenge. They tend to effect many changes in the lives of their parents. It has been said, "Insanity is inherited, and we get it from our children." And although that statement may not be accurate, it seems that way at times.

In dealing with children, it is important to understand what the normal stages of development are. The caregiver needs to be aware that **much can be learned about what a child is struggling with by looking at where they should be in normal development and comparing that with where they are in everyday life.**

Children will begin to **act out their feelings** when they are disturbed or in pain about something. All behavior speaks volumes to an observant person. It is important -- if a child is hyperactive in certain ways, or aggressive toward other children, or dysfunctional in terms of their schoolwork or family relations -- to look at what meaning is behind the non-verbal communication the child is giving. Many times when the child is asked certain questions such as, "How are you?" they will say, "Fine" and they seem to be happy. As their behavior continues to be observed, especially when talking to them about certain themes within the family; ("How's mom?" "How's dad?" "Is there a lot of fighting in your home?" "Does dad drink alcohol?" "Does mom leave you at home alone?") It may create such anxiety in the child that he will begin to act out, even within the caregiving room. The acting out is an indication of how a child is actually functioning in his/her world.

Children's thinking is quite **symbolic**. Because of their lack of verbal skills they are unable to tell anyone directly how they are feeling and experiencing their world. That is why "play therapy," a specialized form of treatment for children, is so powerful and effective. It is important to recognize how Jesus spoke about children and their importance in the world. In the Old Testament children were seen as a **gift from God** and are to be a **joy to their parents**. In the New Testament, Jesus said it would be better for a man to put a weight around his neck and throw himself into the ocean than it would be for him to hurt a little child (Matthew 18:6). Giving care to children requires specialized training. The most important thing a caregiver can do for the child is to **build a relationship of trust**.

Part of the caregiving process with children is to **train the parents on how to deal with what the child is saying about his/her world**. In doing so, hopefully a reorientation of the family system may be brought about so that help and welfare can be provided to the child.

So much more could be said about children and the way children function. Books by James Dobson, Bruce Narramore, and Minirth and Meier are highly recommended.
(See the bibliography)

ADOLESCENTS

Adolescence is not a disease, it just seems like it! The main task with this age group is to **build a solid sense of identity.** Most adolescents are trying to find out who they are, and how they fit into the world. They are also concerned about where they are going with their lives and what they want to do "when they grow up." During this stage of life they are **beginning to separate themselves from the family of origin,** as they are looking forward to becoming a responsible adult in the real world. Their thinking is dual or split. **Part of them wants to be a child and continue to be dependent on the family, while the other part of them desperately wants the freedom to move forward in their life.**

47

The Bible says, "A double minded man is unstable in all of his ways" (James 1:8). No better example of that saying can be found than in the adolescent in action. During the adolescent period there is usually a struggle between peer influence and parent influence. Certain things parents expect of a child under the age of 14 can no longer be expected of a teenager over that age. This can lead to a **power struggle.** Peers usually become more important than parents, but parents remain as the primary influence in the teen's life if they keep communication open. **Good communication** is an imperative when dealing with teenagers. The parents must also be **goal oriented**, realizing the goal is for their adolescent to become a full, functioning member of society and the Body of Christ.

The adolescent needs to have structure and **discipline** as well as a certain amount of **freedom** to be able to grow and to make mistakes in their world.

TEENAGE PREGNANCY AND PARENTING

Teenage pregnancy and parenthood are a major social issue. There are large numbers of young women, age 13 - 19 who become pregnant each year. Approximately 5% of young teenagers in this bracket become pregnant every year. There are major decisions that must be made during this time of crisis. Christians hold strongly to the belief of the sanctity of life. Ruling out abortion, another option is adoption (and all of the subsequent problems). There is also the option of keeping the child, with the related difficulties.

There are significant ways in which the church can help to avoid teenage pregnancy. The training and teaching of young people on the sanctity of marriage and the purpose of human sexuality is a key. The peer pressure on young people to be part of the group, the pressure to experience this exhilarating experience of sexual relations is tremendous. It is very important teenagers be assisted by **being open and candid with them** and teaching them what the Bible says about human sexuality, marriage and family relations.

What should be the response of the church or Christian caregiver to a teenager who becomes pregnant? First of all, it is important to remember that the cause of this is well known. It should not be a shock. Condemnation and shame must be avoided so a rational decision can be made.

Secondly, **pregnancy is not a disease**. It does not make the teenager any less of a worthwhile human being because they have become pregnant. It is important that a teenager be met with a response of **mature, prayerful, grace-filled and loving assistance.**

EATING DISORDERS

Anorexia nervosa. Anorexia is characterized by a **25% weight loss** or a body weight which is 25% below normal. The anorexic has a distorted body image. When anorexics look at themselves in a mirror, they see themselves as fat. They refuse to maintain a weight above a minimum norm for their age and height.

Bulimia nervosa. This eating disorder involves several **binge and purging** episodes several times per week over a period of at least three months. Bulimics will frequently binge and purge and abuse physical exercise. Anorexics usually suffer from more severe psychological and medical problems than will bulimics.

Bulimia and anorexia are quite extensive in the American society. There are up to one half million to five million bulimics and anorexics in the United States. Present estimates state that up to 13% of the adolescent female population are bulimics, 11% are anorexics.

The psychosocial profile of these eating-disordered youngsters includes the concept that they are usually a model child, or a "perfect little princess." Behind this facade is a very poor self-image and a significant need for approval, especially from parents. Many of these teens and young adults are compulsive high achievers. Most of these adolescents **see any form or flaw in their character or body image as a distinct failure which they assume will invite rejection from those who care about them.** They will develop a tremendous sense of anxiety or fear which will dominate every area of their lives.

The **families of most anorexics and bulimics** are typically highly **dependent on each other and cannot handle stress or anger in a positive way.** They are enmeshed; that is, they are overly concerned and involved in each other's lives. There are no clear boundaries developed between individuals in the family.

Paradoxically, the **eating disorder functions to preserve family stability.** The victim secures a sense of identity, approval, and control through the special attention received because of the illness. This requires everyone else to be involved in her life and her illness, and it **helps them to avoid dealing with the real family conflicts that do exist.**

How is this type of crisis to be dealt with? The first step, as with many other problems, is to **confront the denial** in the whole family system.

After confronting the denial, it is then important to **recognize that this is a family problem where a multi-disciplinary approach is needed.** There must be physical needs met through nutrition and sometimes even pervasive medical care. When good treatment occurs, and especially when the power of the Holy Spirit is introduced into the individual's life, over 80% will eventually become binge/purge free.

The following are some guidelines for caregiving with adolescents:

Sincerity. The average adolescent can spot a "phony" in an instant. If an adult doesn't care for them or shows a lack of genuine concern for their needs and wishes, the teenager will simply not relate to them.

Building a relationship. Secondly, the building of a relationship is by far the most important thing to help youth. Adolescents frequently need a friend who can be close to them without exploitation. Once a friendship is established with an adolescent it becomes a relationship that can become dear and precious.

In reality, one can ask anything of an adolescent once they have won their heart. The adolescent will test the relationship in every possible way before they are willing to say, "I trust you."

Part of building the teen's trust is in keeping things **completely confidential** in all dealings with the teen. The caregiver should always **remain the adult**, but be able to recognize that showing care and concern for an adolescent is something he/she desperately needs.

Remember that adolescents are in the midst of **making many choices**. Most of the time, the choices they make are good and positive. It is only a small percentage of teens that end up with great problems. Those who are having trouble need help in making choices utilizing the guidelines of God's Word, logic, and learning patience rather than impulsiveness. Helping adolescents to look at the choices they have and to come up with positive alternatives for them can be of great benefit to the teenager.

CROSS-CULTURAL CAREGIVING

The consideration of a **cross-cultural** perspective requires being aware of the differences people have within their family life based on the cultures in which they have been raised. The average Anglo-Saxon Protestant family has an underlying feeling that **everyone thinks and feels the way they do.** This kind of thinking is naive at best. The truth of the matter is that the majority of the peoples of the world do not think "Western". The mindset in eastern cultures is very different than the mindset of the western cultures. The Hebrew children thought and felt in a more fluid, rounded manner, unlike the Greeks who saw things more in black and white, with few gray areas. Therefore, **in dealing with people from different cultures it is important to understand some of the differences of those cultures.**

The United States, Australia, Canada and other Western nations have become increasingly pluralistic, a proverbial "melting pot" of people. There are still major social problems between the blacks and whites, Orientals and Latinos. The first and even the second generation members of different cultures will think and see the world differently and will have different views and belief systems. They will have different attitudes and ways of solving problems. An example of the differences can be seen in the oriental concept of "saving face" or avoiding "family shame." Whereas in the Hispanic culture there is a strong emphasis on "the male macho man" or as it is called "Machismo." There is a need to **adjust family caregiving methods to the appropriate type of society**. In India, Pakistan, and areas of Africa, time is acknowledged very differently than in America. When a person says, "I'll see you at 3:00," it could mean that they will see you at anywhere from 3:00 to 5:00 or even 7:00 today or perhaps tomorrow. In that part of the world this indifference to time is fairly normal. It can be very frustrating to the person with a western mindset which is, as a rule, very time oriented.

It is highly recommended that a caregiver working in a multi-cultural situation develop relationships and **learn as much as possible about the cultural differences.** The differences can be overcome if the caregiver is not prideful, self-centered, and assumptive; believing all people should think and feel alike, that is, like the caregiver thinks and feels.

CHAPTER VI

SPECIAL CONCERNS

There are many other concerns that a Christian caregiver may face, and provided here are some of the most common problems and types of care that can be provided in a local church setting.

GROUP CAREGIVING AND GROUP DYNAMICS

There are many fine books on group caregiving, a few of which are listed in the list of books for extra reading. The concept of group caregiving is not a new one. The earliest variation is to be found in the New Testament (Acts 2) in the Book of Acts where the first Christians usually met in small groups in someone's home. It has only been during the past decade or two that some of the modern day churches are beginning to see the need for such small groups, usually called home fellowship groups.

Yalom, (1975) in his research with group counseling found there were 11 elements or "curative factors" and he divided them into the following categories:

1. Instillation of hope – the creation of a sense of optimism and positive expectations.
2. Universality -- decreasing each member's sense of being alone in his misery and psychopathology.
3. Imparting of information about mental health and illness.
4. Altruism -- the creation of a group climate of helpfulness, concern, support and sharing.
5. Corrective recapitulation of the primary family group -- helping group members to see that their interactions in the group recapitulate with primary family members.

6. Development of socializing techniques-increasing group members' ability to relate to one another in positive and mature ways.
7. Imitative behavior-helping group members to change via observation and functional, mature behavior on the part of the therapist and other group members.
8. Interpersonal learning -- utilizing transference, corrective emotional experiences, and insight to assist members in changing themselves.
9. Cohesiveness -- the sense of togetherness that causes a group to see itself holistically rather than as a collection of individuals.
10. Catharsis -- the open expression of affect, within the group process.
11. Existential factors -- dealing with such issues as personal responsibility, contingency, basic isolation, and mortality.

BIBLICAL PERSPECTIVE

Although little can be found in the Bible dealing directly with the concept of group caregiving (because the Bible was not written as a book on psychotherapy), it is not too difficult to come to the conclusion that because of the importance of human relationships as discussed earlier in this book, the use of groups in caregiving can be of tremendous value. Such human problems as feelings of isolation, broken relationships, self-esteem, and the many areas of compulsive behavior that tend to generate great guilt, can be handled best in the group situation.

GROUP LEADERSHIP

Anyone entertaining the idea of becoming a group leader should take the time to read as much as possible on the subject of effective leadership styles and should take as many seminars and training sessions as possible. The entire subject of leadership is beyond the limits of this book.

It should be noticed that there are different styles of leadership. The two that are included here present such a challenge that the reader is directed to consider both types for further study. The two styles are: 1. directive and 2. non-directive. Their very titles describe the style. In directive leadership the leader of the group sets the standards and dictates the direction the group will take, while the non-directive leader is more of a facilitator of what is taking place naturally within the group. It is generally agreed in group caregiving that the most effective leadership style of the two is the non-directive.

GUILT AND FORGIVENESS

Lewis Smedes stated that forgiveness is more a process than an event. The need for the receiving of forgiveness from God and others is quite evident to most Christians. Yet in spite of the apparent need to be relieved of guilt, and to receive forgiveness, many Christians struggle in this area.

GUILT DEFINED

Guilt can be either **objective** or **subjective** in nature. Objective guilt can refer to a person's condition in relation to a human law or to God. Subjective guilt is divided into self-condemning emotions called pseudo or false guilt, and love based corrective feelings such as constructive sorrow.

When an individual comes to caregiving with a load of guilt, it is important to determine which type of guilt is being expressed. How the symptoms of guilt are treated is determined by an accurate assessment.

When dealing with objective guilt, that is when a **sin against God or the violation of a human law** is the case, the client must become aware of his/her need for salvation, forgiveness, and to make restitution for the law breaking. The only provision for true forgiveness was made by Jesus Christ on the cross.

Pseudo guilt or false guilt, the subjective guilt, is usually more difficult to deal with. The difficulty comes not due to the severity of past offenses, but to the inability of the client to release himself from accountability for the offense. The reasons for this are many and the primary ones are discussed below:

1. **Unconfessed sin.** Obviously, if the counselee has sin in his/her life that has never been confessed (I John 1:9), then forgiveness cannot be received.

2. **Condemnation.** Condemnation and conviction are not the same thing. Condemnation or the putting down and shaming of oneself for past wrongs; is either from the devil, from oneself, or from other people. In any case, condemnation can lead to depression and immobilization if not properly dealt with.

In working with a person who is troubled by guilt and condemnation, the talking/confession process is most helpful (James 5). The counselee must be willing to share in depth the hurts of their life. An accepting attitude is of primary importance. Sharing scripture is important but not to the point of bludgeoning the client and bringing greater condemnation (Rom. 8:1).

The caregiver must help the client process through to the place of forgiveness. That is:
1. **Express** the anger, hurt, or fear regarding the incidents that the client feels condemnation for and placing responsibility (not blame) where it belongs.
2. Develop a new perspective on the meaning of past events.
3. Receive God's forgiveness and release others from responsibility.

4. Give thanks to the Lord for this release and develop strategies to go on with life without the guilt and condemnation.

As mentioned before, resolving guilt and condemnation is not an event, but rather a process.

GRIEF AND LOSS

The following is a summary of the topic of dealing with grief.

Grief is categorized into three primary areas of loss. Those areas are:
1. Loss in the area of **relationship.**
2. Loss in the area of **events or situations.**
3. Loss in the area of **self or personal loss as in identity.**

Relationship losses are those losses that may occur naturally or sometimes catastrophically in the course of an individual's life. One example of this type of loss would be the **loss of a loved animal.**

Another level of loss that occurs often in relationships is the loss of a **close friend.** Friendships, for many people, are very difficult to come by and are very powerful and important. When a close friend is lost, whether through death, separation, or just through time and circumstances, it can be a painful process. Some people just do not do well in saying "Good-bye" to friendships.

The third area of grief has to do with the loss of relationships as in the **separation of husband and wife.** This separation may be the result of the military deployment of either the man or the woman. The problems of separation in military families are a study of its own. But here also, the individuals need to learn to be able to say, "Good-bye" in a way that will minimize the trauma to all parties involved (husband, wife and, especially children).

There are **other forms** of separation in this relational situation such as **divorce, debilitating sickness, and death**. All of these kinds of separation carry with them a different degree of grief, but the handling of that grief is similar to the other losses in life.

In this same area, the **loss of children** in one form or another must be considered. There is a time, especially for women, that psychologists call the empty nest syndrome. For women the roles of mother and wife are usually very important to their sense of identity. When the children finally grow up and approach the time for them to leave the home (nest) the mother experiences a sense of loss, not only because of the absence of the children, but because of the sudden loss of a part of her purpose in life after spending so many years taking care of her charges. Many women experience an identity crisis which leads to depression and other psychological problems. The process of saying "Good-bye" to children is one that needs to be consciously dealt with. It should be a part of the family planning and should be discussed often with the children.

It is important to be able to recognize the feelings of separation and to realize there is going to be a certain amount of sadness and hurt that will need to be dealt with in the caregiving situation.

Divorce was mentioned as one form of separation that produces a sense of loss, but there is a further problem to be dealt with in this area. Not only is divorce a difficult topic for most people to discuss, but it creates special problems in the Evangelical Christian community. It has been found that divorce occurs almost as often in the Evangelical Christian community as it does in the community at large. Divorce is an extremely painful time for people to experience, and they need all of the loving, caring help of a good caregiver during the process of divorce and for some time after.

In the caregiving of divorce victims, it is necessary to recognize many negative feelings such as anger, resentment, bitterness, and hurt that will need to be addressed in the caregiving office. Unless those negative feelings are resolved and the client is finally able to say that "good-bye" he will most likely carry the negativity into the next relationship. It is important to be able to say a final "good-bye" before being able to say a meaningful "hello" in the new relationship.

Other areas of loss include:
1. **A sense of the loss of one's youth.** This sense of loss is compounded by the field of commercial advertisement that places so much emphasis on youth and beauty. For men it is usually an emphasis on athletic ability or virility.
2. **A loss in the area of job or occupational loss.** The work ethic that has for as long as one can remember been that the man of the house is the "bread winner" and is less of a man if he cannot care for the needs of his family. In modern times this problem has been extended to women as well.

Stages of Grief

There are six classic stages of grief people will naturally process through. They do so at their own pace or timing but will finally process through each. The modification of the stages is derived from original research conducted by Elizabeth Kubler-Ross, On Death and Dying. (1969). the six stages include:
1. **Shock** -- nature's way of insulating one from the pain of loss.
2. **Denial** -- the normal inability to fully accept the loss. This is a normal process unless it continues for a significant time period.
3. **Fantasy Vs Reality** -- akin to denial, the individual struggles with memories, and feelings of the person lost.

4. **Release** -- finally, the emotions begin to flow, with the subsequent mixture of feelings. This should be encouraged but not dwelt upon.
5. **Living with Memories** -- adjusting with the fact of the loss, putting relationships (both good and bad) into perspective.
6. **Acceptance, affirmation** -- completing the cycle without denying the loss, yet embracing or affirming life in its fullness.

The Bible says man is "fearfully and wonderfully made." The Word also says the "heart is deceitfully wicked. Who can know it?" Grief is experienced in the self, or the soul, that God has created. A loss can be devastating to the sense of self-esteem. Loss which leads to grief can **leave man in a state of bitterness and despair** if not dealt with, leaving the individual vulnerable to the works of the enemy and to the works of the person's own flesh or soul. It is vital, both as Christians and as human beings in general, to learn to deal with the multitude of losses that are going to be experienced in a lifetime. The Apostle Paul said after having gone through peril, distress, and all kinds of difficulties, he was always "more than a conqueror." In spite of all the losses he experienced, he was able to deal with them and to say "good-bye," and "...forgetting what is behind and straining toward what is ahead, **I press on** toward the goal to win the prize for which God has called me heavenward in Christ Jesus" (Phil. 3:13-14 NIV). This is the goal of all Christians.

DEPRESSION

Of all the maladies a caregiver may face perhaps **the most common one of all is depression.** Depression, in all of its forms (from mild to debilitating) can cause serious problems for the individual experiencing it and for the caregiver treating it.

The primary symptoms of depression include feelings of **intense sadness, discouragement** and a **lack of energy or zest for life.** Further symptoms include:

1. **Physical.** Troubled sleep, weight loss, or gain, lack of interest in sex or food.

2. **Thought Processes.** Tend to be quite negative and self abasing, with a general outlook of doom and gloom. At the extremes, these negative thought patterns can become quite self-destructive, even suicidal.

3. **Affective.** The emotions of the depressed person can range from hopelessness and guilt to fear and agitation. These emotions can manifest themselves in crying, or by inconsistent or inappropriate behavior within the social setting.

4. **Motor Activity.** Motor activity is often slowed, which may include social withdrawal, decrease in general work performance and general lethargy.

In the caregiving situation, it is important to recognize how **vulnerable** the counselee is. Their normal ways of coping with difficulties are no longer working. It is important to take the concerns of a depressed person seriously, especially with regard to suicidal expressions.

In treating depression, the first step is to determine its roots. It is often advisable to have a physician or psychologist examine the client for possible biological (endogenous) factors for the depression. In cases of biological problems, medication may be most helpful and appropriate. Properly prescribed medication can alleviate suffering and speed the healing process. If there is no clear biological component, it is important to look for the roots in the following areas:

1. **Physical problems.** In women, childbirth, menstruation, medication, drugs and alcohol problems may cause depression.

2. **Relationships.** Severe loss or disappointment in relationships with significant others such as husband, wife, children or individuals at the work place.

3. **Financial Problems.** Financial problems can indicate specific problems, especially when the financial problems are caused by such behavioral problems as gambling, alcoholism, etc.

4. **Social Isolation.** Social isolation is one of the chief issues faced in the caregiving situation .It is characterized by withdrawal, self-pity and loneliness. Depressives will often "yes, but" the caregiver into considerable frustration if they are allowed to do so.

Ministering to those who are depressed is challenging. Because of their lack of energy and sense of hopelessness, gaining insight as to the underlying causes for the depression can be difficult for both the caregiver and the counselee. Therefore, a **behavioral approach** in the beginning is usually best as the counselee is unraveling their story for the caregiver. This approach can include (besides a good physical exam) walking, change of diet, listening to worshipful music, reading the Word of God, etc. The primary focus in the beginning will be to evaluate the client and give hope. A helper (someone from the church family) may be needed who can assist the client with their "homework."

A secondary focus with this kind of person is to maintain **a non-judgmental style** while exploring the underlying reasons, helping the client express any repressed feelings and seeking forgiveness. Often the client's depression is rooted in anger, resentment or bitterness, which must be resolved through confession, prayer and repentance.

Finally, **reorientation of the thinking process** (from negative to Godly, realistic) is necessary. The client must become aware of negative thoughts in their inner dialogue that are self-condemning, and focus instead on the truth of God's Word. Since the Word of God **does penetrate into the depths of the soul**, and **since it has power to transform,** speaking the truth to oneself is very important. **Only a complete renewal of the mind will "cure" depression that is not organically based.**

Depression can be overcome. It takes a long process, but with patience and prayer, effective changes can occur.

HUMAN SEXUALITY

Human sexuality is a gift from God to man from the very beginning of man's existence (Genesis 1:26-28 and Genesis 2:18-25). Sex was God's plan for the 1) **procreation of humans** after the first two, Adam and Eve, were created by Him. With the exception of Jesus, every other man came from the sexual union of a man and a woman in the act of sex. Not only did God ordain that man would be born of woman through the act of sexual union, but the Lord also ordained that sex should be for 2) **pleasure and mutual satisfaction** for both the man and the woman. It is God, himself, that said that the two, man and woman, would become one flesh as a very intimate component of human interaction.

It is an amazing fact that many of the problems men and women experience, psychologically, physiologically and spiritually stem from difficulties in the area of sex and sexual relations. As human sexuality is largely learned (sexual drives, etc. are physiological) from interactions with other human beings, first the parents and then significant others in the persons environment, it is understandable that many problems can occur, because of wrong thinking, sinful lusts, ignorant or uninformed parental examples, etc.

Only a few of the major problems in the area of human sexuality will be considered in this book. With many of these problems and some of the more complex abnormalities a caregiver may face in the caregiving situation, it would be the better part of wisdom to refer such problems to a professional who deals primarily with difficulties in this sensitive field.

SOME PROBLEMS THAT OCCUR IN THE AREA OF HUMAN SEXUALITY

Caregivers should become aware of and be willing to do further reading on the following problems as a minimum preparation as a pastoral or lay caregiver:

1. **Physiological problems.** Inability to have proper functioning due to physical causes, such as:
   a. **Diabetes**: Number one cause of impotency in males.
   b. **Obesity**: makes sex uncomfortable and difficult.
   c. **Tipped uterus**: results in painful intercourse.

2. **Male problems: Impotence**
   a. **Primary** - could be physiological, but usually is not. The inability to have a full erection ever is very rare.
   b. **Secondary** - able to have an erection, but can't sustain erection or experiences premature ejaculation.

3. **Female Problems**:
   a. **Vaginismus** - spasmodic contraction of the vagina (is painful - clamps down/closure and prevents the penetration of the penis). This is usually a physiological disorder...

b. **Dyspareunia** - painful intercourse of any kind. It could be physiological or psychological. It may be caused by a tumor, scarring or tipping of the uterus.
4. **Problems experienced by both male and female.**
   a. **Lack of sexual desire** - Not physiological but has physical symptoms. Some lose the desire because they set an age in their minds that they think the desire should end and the desire consequently does diminish at that age.

It is common for caregivers to encounter some problems that can best be thought of as spiritual **problems**. These problems may include:
1. **Lustful thinking**
2. **Adultery** (pornea) and sexual immorality in general outside the marriage.
3. **Immorality**
4. **Homosexuality**

In the marital setting, all sexual problems are related; they are symptoms of a dysfunctional marital relationship. So when dealing with sexual problems in marriage, **the marriage relationship must be the focus of attention**. The caregiver needs to find out what each partner wants out of the sexual relationship and what the difficulties are at the present time. The caregiver can learn a lot by taking a sexual history. Such questions as, "From whom did you learn about sex?" and, "What were the attitudes of your family about sex?" should be asked.

TREATMENT OF SEXUAL PROBLEMS

Although there are a number of recommended exercises that can be recommended to a married couple who are having problems of a sexual nature, it seems advisable the caregiver should obtain some books (preferably Christian in content) and become very familiar with the material before attempting to recommend any such specific exercises to the couple. However, there are some general things that can be readily recommended to a couple to help them if lack of sexual desire or lack of education appear to be the major cause of their difficulties.

1. Go out on **dates** (that is with each other, of course). Women need romance. We are told that women often assent to sex in order to get romance, whereas, men give romance in order to receive sex. It is also helpful to give the couple a neutral topic to talk about on dates so that they can begin to build bridges in their relationship.
2. **Paradoxical Intention** -- Here the caregiver suggests that the couple abstain from sex all week, which is just the opposite of the goal.

Most often the problems faced by couples are the result of **faulty education or selfishness.** It is in this area that caregivers can do the most good. It is amazing how little some people know about the whole subject of sexual relations. It is also very revealing to discover how much misinformation there is to be found in the thinking of many people. Some of the misinformation may have come from the unresolved problems of the family of origin. Further, with self-centered attitudes, direct biblical application becomes quite difficult.

The caregiver must develop spiritual maturity in dealing with sexual problems, especially problems of an addictive nature (See Matt. 9:20, 21, 22-30). It is important that the client be **willing to be healed**. In Romans 10:17 it is suggested there is also a need of faith.

Above all else the caregiver needs to be supportive. The client needs to learn to trust the caregiver with mutual love and respect. **The caregiver should not attempt to deal with a sexual problem with which they are not themselves comfortable.**

Here is one final word about sexual addictions. There are usually several phases to sexual addiction that the caregiver needs to understand.

1. **Tension**
2. **Anxiety, shame, or guilt** - (Such as Adam and Eve experienced)
3. **Release**
4. **Despair** - leads to depression, etc. The client develops a belief system that they cannot break the habit and they don't know the source. A variation of the A.A. 12 step program can be helpful in dealing with this disorder.

CHILD ABUSE

The subject of the treatment of child abuse is a book in itself. However, the following suggestions should be helpful for the pastoral or lay caregiver. In the role of a caregiver, a report of child abuse must be made immediately to the proper authorities. Child abuse can take on many forms. A child may be abused physically, sexually, verbally, or by neglect. The more physical forms of abuse are much easier to identify than verbal abuse or abuse by neglect, but the harm to the child can be equally as damaging in any form of abuse

Many of the following suggestions can be used for parents under stress, but who have not acted out to hurt their children.

1. Assist the client in developing coping skills and emotional expression.
2. By tying the past with the present, the caregiver can help the client resolve some of the conflicts that are the source of the problem the parent is experiencing in the abuse of their child. This process can be called **effective parenting**.
3. Assist the client in learning:
   a. to show **praise and positive** responses to the child

    b.   effective **discipline** through the use of such concepts as logical consequences (punishment fits the crime) and "Time-out," times to allow for a period of cooling off.
    c.   to **selectively ignore** wrong behavior at times.

The symptoms of child abuse may include some or all of the following:

1. The child may be observed to be **acting out** when abuse is happening.
2. The child may **withdraw** from family and others.
3. The child will most likely experience low self-esteem.
4. The child may engage in **promiscuous behavior.**
5. The child may **run away,** have problems at school, etc.

From the viewpoint of the child, they will usually consider themselves to blame for what is happening. They will usually see themselves as "bad." They see the bad parent and provider, and when the parent is reported, the child will experience a sense of loss.

All things considered, the caregiver must realize that, for the sake and safety of the child, he/she must be separated from the family of origin, if abuse is occurring. Separating the child from the family brings up placement issues such as:

1. The **child's safety and personal needs** come first.
2. The caregiver really has no control over the process. By law in most states, it is the prerogative of the state to **literally take over** in cases of child abuse.
3. Because the process of healing for the child abuser is a long one, the **child will probably be placed in a foster home**, and possibly never be reunited with the real parents.
4. In some cases, when treatment is effective there may be a **reunification of the family.**

There are many indicators that a caregiver can look for in discovering abuse, and the reader is referred to the book "Family Violence" by this author.

Jan Frank has developed a fine treatment program for sufferers of abuse, especially incest, in a book called A Door of Hope published, in 1983 by Here's Life Pub. I have outlined her key steps here.

1. Face the Problem (I Cor. 11:28)
2. Recount the Incident (Nehemiah 2)
3. Experience the Feelings (Nehemiah 2)
4. Establish the Responsibilities (Joshua 7; Hosea 2:14, 15)
5. Trace the Behavioral Difficulties/Symptoms.
6. Observe Others/Educate Self-Confront the Aggressor (Matthew 18:15)
7. Acknowledge Forgiveness (Col. 3:13)
8. Rebuild Self-image and Relationships (Nehemiah 4:17)
9. Express Concern and Empathize with Others (II Cor. 1:3, 4)

Again, it cannot be emphasized too strongly the need for as much education and training in the area of human sexuality as possible. The pastor or lay caregiver can cause more problems than he cures if situations involving sexual problems, especially child molestation are not handled in a strictly professional way.

LEGAL AND ETHICAL ISSUES IN THE CAREGIVING MINISTRY

Definitions

LEGAL: Laws that have been passed for the protection of human beings by government officials, whether national, state, or local.

ETHICAL ISSUES: What a prudent man would decide to do given a certain situation he is facing.

Some of the legal and/or ethical issues in regard to the caregiving ministry are discussed here.

THE DUTY TO WARN: In the state of California there is a state-mandated law for licensed psychotherapists to warn if a person they are counseling may be a danger to someone else. **A** caregiver has an ethical responsibility to contact the person who is in danger, whenever possible. Secondly, to make contact with a protective agency such as the police, if someone is in danger. An example of the kind of thing that should be reported is a counselee threatening to commit murder. It is recommended that Christian caregivers have a supervisory relationship with a professional counselor to assist with handling situations such as this.

DUTY TO REPORT: In cases of child abuse, and in some cases of elder abuse, the Christian caregiver has a duty to report to the proper authorities. Lay caregivers should consult their supervisor /pastor prior to making the report.

CONFIDENTIALITY
The protection of the personal life of your counselee is a primary responsibility of the caregiver. This includes how you talk about your counselee (if at all) and the protection of records (others or yours) written about the client.

Information about the client and their personal life, especially as discussed in the caregiving session, are privileged communication. That is, only the client has the right to discuss the contents of their life unless they give permission to the caregiver to do so (on an individual basis) and preferably in writing. The caregiver is never to discuss the contents of the client's communication without the client's consent. This includes church leadership, unless this is cleared (again in writing) with the client prior to or at the beginning of formal caregiving. Nothing will destroy a caregiving ministry faster than if a client believes their personal life may be shared with outsiders.

Also, the records of the client's life, including your notes, should be protected and kept safe from review by outsiders. Keeping the records locked in a file cabinet behind a locked office door is deemed the minimum protection needed.

Under certain circumstances, information can be released, such as to other professionals. A written permission should be obtained from the client before releasing (or obtaining) information. Whether medical records, school records, legal records or the like; written permission should be obtained and kept safely in the client's file.

MAKING REFERRALS
Knowing when to refer to other professionals is a very important issue in caregiving. The Christian caregiver must recognize all caregivers are limited in their capabilities, gifts and skills. When dealing with a client whose problem is beyond the expertise of the caregiver, the ethical and moral responsibility of the caregiver is to refer. It is usually advisable to refer to other professionals in the community. Therefore, each Christian caregiver should develop a network of resources to which clients may be referred. Individual caregiving may be helpful when dealing with someone struggling with substance abuse, but many times these clients may need an inpatient setting such as a hospital or treatment center, or they may

need additional support from AA, NA, or related Christian programs.

It is a matter of greatest importance that the pastoral or lay caregiver knows when to refer an individual to someone with a higher level of competence or training. There are basically two conditions under which a client should be referred. They are:
1. When a person's needs surpass the time available from the pastor or lay caregiver.
2. When the individual's needs surpass the caregivers expertise such as some of the following situations:
   a. Psychotics.
   b. Depression with severe suicide ideation. When intensity, duration, and complexity of symptoms suggest deeper problems.
   c. When there are possible physiological components or causes.
   d. When there are no structures of consultation and supervision.

DEMONOLOGY AND INNER HEALING

Scriptures do not speak about possession in the same way that the word is used in modern day language. The actual words in the Greek translated to present day English as "demon possession" referred to someone who is "demonized." **Demon activity or possession does not occur in the <u>spirit</u> of man but rather in the <u>soul</u> or the <u>body.</u>** That is to say a person can become "demonized" even though they are born again and Spirit filled. **Christians can still be influenced by demonic attack.** Demons are, in fact, enemies of God, spirit beings with personality and motivation. Their personality is one of total dementia, that is, they are **completely demented** without the possibility of regeneration. Their motivation is to destroy the saints of God. John 10:10 says, "the thief cometh not but to kill, steal and to destroy."

Through the sins and weaknesses of parents or through a person's own sinful acts demonic influence can require the ministry of **deliverance** as a means of setting someone free from demonic influence. The Lord intended the soul, the mind, will, and emotions, as well as the body, to be under the complete control of the spirit and man's spirit to be completely under the control of the Holy Spirit.

When an individual is born again his spirit comes to life, but the soul is still under the influence of the old nature and needs to be restored and regenerated. The process of restoration and regeneration takes time. In dealing with this kind of problem it is of great importance that the Christian have the gift of **discernment** as well as considerable wisdom and knowledge about the whole topic of demonology.

The Word of God indicates, without reservation, that the warfare that occurs in human lives is a **spiritual warfare**, not a physical or psychological warfare. The warfare for our lives occurs **within the mind**. 2 Corinthians 10:5 talks about this warfare very clearly. The scripture teaches that Christians must be willing to "cast down imaginations and every high and lofty thought **that exalts itself against the knowledge of God** and to bring **every** thought captive into the obedience of Christ." .

The renewal, or the regeneration, of the mind comes through the **washing of the water by the Word of God** (Ephesians 5:26). Because so much conflict occurs in the body and the mind, it is easy to see how a person can be under demonic influences.

The following summary of the process of deliverance from the occult, or from demonic activity is followed by a look at the ministry of the healing of the memories from a balanced Christian view point, in an effort to "debunk" some of the myths of this process.

The Word of God discusses various occult practices, including:

1. **Enchantments** or the practice of magical arts. See Exodus 7:11-22, Leviticus 19:26, Deuteronomy 18:10, Daniel 1:20.
2. **Witchcraft**, which is the sin of rebellion, the practice of dealing with evil spirits. See: Exodus 22:18, Deuteronomy 18:9-10, 1 Samuel 15:23, 2 Kings 9:22, Nahum 3:4 and Galatians 5:19-21. All of these activities are forbidden by God.
3. **Sorcery**, which is similar to witchcraft except drugs are used. See: Exodus 7:11, Isaiah 47:9, Jeremiah 27:9, Malachi 3:5, Acts 8:9-11, Revelation 9:21.
4. **Soothsaying** or telling the future by demonic power. See: Isaiah 2:6, Daniel 2:27, 4:7, Micah 5:12.
5. **Divination** is the art of mystic insight or fortune telling, sometimes with demon power. See: Numbers 22:7, 23:23, Deuteronomy 18:10-14.

In ministering to someone that has been actively involved in the occult, it is important to recognize the **problems being dealt with are substantial. The caregiver must be willing to stand up to the enemy and not to be manipulated by him.** The caregiver should never lose sight of the fact that the Word of God is the sword of the Spirit and is a strong weapon in dealing with demonic activities.

When a person comes in for caregiving it is important to **first discover whether they have been involved in any sort of demonic activity.** Through careful and discerning questioning the caregiver can discover whether there are areas such as witchcraft, drug abuse, sexual abuse, etc., which have been a part of the counselee's lifestyle

Ministering deliverance to individuals is nothing more or less than **commanding that the demonic force that is working against the individual be broken in the Name of Jesus.**

However, the minister must be careful and protective toward people in the caregiving situation and never to be exploitive.

In dealing with the **healing of memories** there are many things to be aware of. First of all, caregivers need to realize healing of the memories is a **valid form of ministry**. 1 Corinthians 12:28 it talks about the gift of healing. There is also a gift of "healings." There are many forms of healings including physical healing, healing through the Lord's Supper, and healing through the laying on of hands. There is also the natural healing found in nature. **The human body has a built in system whereby over a period of time many ailments are healed without any particular interference or help from any outside source**. Healing was provided in the death of Christ. The Scripture says that "by His stripes we all were healed" (Isa. 53:5; I Peter 2:24).

There are times when healing will come through the caregiving process. As mentioned in another section of this book, many physical ailments are psychosomatic: a physical sickness that has been caused by a psychological condition such as stress, anxiety, etc. With the proper loving counsel of a Christian caregiver the psychological source of the problems can be eliminated resulting in the healing of the **physical problem**. Many people receive healing of the memories, mind, will and emotions through the relational process of **growing** in the things of God, through studying the Word of God, through being in **relationship with other Christians**, and through **prayer and confession of sins**. A look at the process of inner healing should prove helpful.

The **process of inner healing** cannot really occur unless an individual is willing to **open the door to their unconscious mind**. Many people suffer from problems in their lives, yet are unaware of the source of the problems. Not every memory needs to be remembered. Only those that are truly problematic need to be dealt with. The Apostle Paul talked about forgetting, or **putting off, the past**, but many times a person needs to **first remember**

that which needs to be put off before it can truly be "put off." It is the ministry of the Holy Spirit to help individuals remember those things too painful to remember without His help. Therefore, the **client must learn to trust the Holy Spirit in the process of inner healing. The Holy Spirit will lead into all truth <u>if He is allowed to.</u>** See: (2 Corinthians 1:21-22.).

It is necessary to recognize that because of wounds or injuries in the mind, will and emotions of man, denial and repression may occur. When a child is injured by a traumatic event beyond his ability to understand, the memory of the event will be repressed out of consciousness, but it is never completely forgotten. It is the responsibility of the caregiver to assist the counselee through the help of the Holy Spirit to get in touch with the memories so they can be healed.

Robert McDonald, in his book on memory healing, describes a process for inner healing that has proven to be very powerful and effective. He first describes the **setting.** The setting for inner healing should be **private, safe,** and **confidential.** A condition of relaxation, trust, openness, and caring must be set, and the Holy Spirit invited to begin to reveal areas of people's lives. The second stage begins when such a condition is set and there is a lessening of resistance so that God begins to move powerfully on behalf of the client.

The process of inner healing takes time. This second stage does not usually fit into the standard caregiving hour. The minimum recommended time is **1 1/2 to 2 hours** for this purpose.

Teaching is a third stage which actually is the beginning part of the inner healing process. The individual needs to be taught what he/she is about to experience. Simply stated, the caregiver will inform the counselee "we are going to pray first, ask the Holy Spirit to begin to reveal to us areas of your life that need to be revealed and healed." It is important that all sin be confessed so no further damage can occur.

The fourth stage of inner healing involves **every memory being prayed over as it is brought up**. The memory may come in terms of a **trace memory.** It may come in forms of a sensation or a **symptom** of some sort. The caregiver prays, first of all, leading the client in a confession if there is sin or a renunciation of vows that were taken in that are forbidden in God's Word. Next, the Holy Spirit is asked to begin to minister in that area, and then Jesus is asked to forgive and to cleanse by His blood of any sin or wrong. Now the prayer for healing can begin. At times the laying on of hands will be helpful, but at all times the fervent effective prayer of the righteous man will avail much. (James 5:16).

Finally, it is important for the clients to have a support system of people who will pray with them, believe God for them, and give them great support during the time of healing.

Christian caregivers must be strong in the Lord and the power of His might and recognize the need to operate **in His authority,** especially in recognition of the fact that Satan is turning loose his demonic forces to wreak havoc among individuals and families.

Conclusion

Christian care giving is an important area of ministry in support of local church life. It is not for the faint in heart, and much skill is needed. My prayer is that you will do what is required to become the most effective care giver for the sake of others in the body of Christ.

BIBLIOGRAPHY

Clinebell, Howard.   Basic Types of Pastoral Care and Caregiving.
Nashville: Abingdon Press. 1990.

Crabb, Larry.   Effective Biblical Caregiving. Grand Rapids:
Zondervan 1977.

DeKoven, Stan.   Journey to Wholeness: Restoration of the Soul.
Ramona: Vision Publishing. 1988.

DeKoven, Stan.   Grief Relief. Ramona: Vision Publishing. 1988.

DeKoven, Stan. I Want to Be Like You, Dad.. Ramona: Vision
Publishing. 1993.

DeKoven, Stan. Family Violence: Patterns of Destruction, Vision
Publishing, 1998

Frank, Jan. A Door of Hope. Placenta: Here's Life Publishers.
1983.

Gilbert, Marvin and Brock, Raymond T.   The Holy Spirit and
Caregiving. Mass Hendrickson. 1985.

Kubler-Ross, Elizabeth. On Death and Dying. Macmillian. 1970.

Sartir, Virginia. Conjoint Family Therapy. Science and Behavior.
1982

Smedes, Lewis. Forgive and Forget. New York: Harper Row, Inc.
1984.

Sweeton, Gary. Unpublished Seminar Notes.

Yolom, <u>Group Psychotherapy.</u> 1975.
Wright, H. Norman, (1985) Crisis <u>Caregiving: Helping People in Crisis and Stress.</u> Here's Life Publications.

About the Author

Dr. Stan DeKoven is the founder and President of Vision International Ministries, with programs including:

- Vision International University
- Vision International Education Network, with Learning Centers in over 150 nations worldwide.
- Vision Publishing
- Walk in Wisdom Ministries
- International Association of Christian Counseling Professionals

Further, Dr. DeKoven is the author of over 35 books and guides in practical Christian living, all of which are an outgrowth of his extensive teaching ministry both nationally and internationally.

Dr. DeKoven is a graduate of San Diego State University, (B.A. Psychology), Webster University' (M.A. Counseling), Professional School of Psychological Studies (Ph.D., Counseling Psychology) Evangelical Theological Seminary (D.Min.) and is a licensed Marriage, Family and Child Counselor. As an Ordained minister and professional caregiver and educator, he is actively establishing educational programs and counseling ministry around the world and **equipping** God's leaders to equip the saints for end-time harvest.